GREATER THAN A TOURIST- CYPRUS

(TRAVEL GUIDE BOOK FROM A LOCAL)

50 Travel Tips from a Local

Chrissie Stephen

Cover Template Creator: Lisa Rusczyk Ed. D. using Canva.
Cover Creator: Lisa Rusczyk Ed. D.
Image: https://pixabay.com/en/boat-harbor-fishing-shelter-sea-2080222/

CZYK Publishing Since 2011.

Greater Than a Tourist
Visit our website at www.GreaterThanaTourist.com

Lock Haven, PA
ISBN: 9781798400241

>TOURIST

50 TRAVEL TIPS FROM A LOCAL

BOOK DESCRIPTION

Are you excited about planning your next trip?

Do you want to try something new?

Would you like some guidance from a local?

If you answered yes to any of these questions, then this Greater Than a Tourist book is for you.

Greater Than a Tourist- Cyprus by Chrissie Stephen offers the inside scoop on Cyprus. Most travel books tell you how to travel like a tourist. Although there is nothing wrong with that, as part of the Greater Than a Tourist series, this book will give you travel tips from someone who has lived at your next travel destination.

In these pages, you will discover advice that will help you throughout your stay. This book will not tell you exact addresses or store hours but instead will give you excitement and knowledge from a local that you may not find in other smaller print travel books.

Travel like a local. Slow down, stay in one place, and get to know the people and the culture. By the time you finish this book, you will be eager and prepared to travel to your next destination.

Inside this travel guide book you will find:

- Insider tips from a local.

- A bonus book *50 Things to Know About Packing Light for Travel* by bestselling author Manidipa Bhattacharyya.

- Packing and planning list.

- List of travel questions to ask yourself or others while traveling.

- A place to write your travel bucket list.

OUR STORY

Traveling is a passion of the "Greater than a Tourist" series creator. Lisa studied abroad in college, and for their honeymoon Lisa and her husband toured Europe. During her travels to Malta, an older man tried to give her some advice based on his own experience living on the island since he was a young boy. She was not sure if she should talk to the stranger but was interested in his advice. When traveling to some places she was wary to talk to locals because she was afraid that they weren't being genuine. Through her travels, Lisa learned how much locals had to share with tourists. Lisa created the *Greater Than a Tourist* book series to help connect people with locals. A topic that locals are very passionate about sharing.

TABLE OF CONTENTS

DEDICATION

This book is dedicated to my husband John, Claire, Ian, Lara and all my wonderful friends in Cyprus.

ABOUT THE AUTHOR

For more than 23 years, Chrissie Stephen (née Flint) lived in Cyprus with her family. It really was 'love at first sight' when they first arrived and were driven from the airport through the citrus groves with the fruit glistening in the winter sunshine and the fragrance being almost intoxicating.

Chrissie loved living in Cyprus and the warmth and hospitality of its people. She worked as a writer and radio presenter and her interest in the traditions of the country took her to the smallest villages where time seems to have stood still and the days and weeks are measured by the passing seasons rather than the clock.

Cyprus is a great place to visit all year through and there is something of interest for all ages. For Chrissie, the magic of Cyprus begins as you step out of the aircraft and smell the distinctive fragrance of the island's wild herbs…

HOW TO USE THIS BOOK

The *Greater Than a Tourist* book series was written by someone who has lived in an area for over three months. The goal of this book is to help travelers either dream or experience different locations by providing opinions from a local. The author has made suggestions based on their own experiences. Please do your own research before traveling to the area in case the suggested places are unavailable.

Travel Advisories: As a first step in planning any trip abroad, check the Travel Advisories for your intended destination.
https://travel.state.gov/content/travel/en/traveladvisories/traveladvisories.html

FROM THE PUBLISHER

Traveling can be one of the most important parts of a person's life. The anticipation and memories that you have are some of the best. As a publisher of the Greater Than a Tourist book series, as well as the popular *50 Things to Know* book series, we strive to help you learn about new places, spark your imagination, and inspire you. Wherever you are and whatever you do I wish you safe, fun, and inspiring travel.

Lisa Rusczyk Ed. D.
CZYK Publishing

WELCOME TO
> TOURIST

Situated in the eastern Mediterranean, the island of Cyprus enjoys more than 330 days of sunshine each year – making it ideal for holidays all year through! The island has a rich and colourful history stretching back 10, 000 years. It is a small island with a diverse topography which includes mountain ranges, two salt lakes and numerous beaches. This diversity means that Cyprus is rich in birds, flowers, butterflies and trees and offers an excellent range of sports and other activities for all ages.

Cyprus is located between the continents of Europe, Africa and Asia and with its extensive network of international flights it is a popular conference destination. Beautiful scenery and romantic choice of venues have made Cyprus one of the top ten wedding destinations. Sadly, since July 1974, Cyprus has been a divided island and this guide is about the Republic of Cyprus and lets you into 50 secrets as to why it makes the perfect travel destination...

1. STEP INTO YESTERDAY...

It is well worth visiting Nicosia if you have the chance. It is a small capital city with a wonderful blend of wide pavements and narrow twisting alleys, smart fashion shops, street cafés, and interesting museums. The Old City is situated within the Venetian star-shaped city walls and the area known as 'Laiki Yitonia' – the 'peoples' neighbourhood' is a collection of shops and workshops that have been handed down through the generations! In Laiki Yitonia, you will find tailors who can make suits in days, shoemakers, lace makers and coppersmiths too and their skills contrast sharply with the big new stores in the modern part of Nicosia, selling all the big names at attractive prices.

2. GETTING A GRIP OF THE CYPRUS PROBLEM

Whilst in Old Nicosia, it is easy to come across 'the Green Line' which is patrolled by soldiers from the United Nations and is what makes Nicosia a divided city. It is now possible on production of ID to cross over into the Turkish part of the city and to understand the sad events of 1974, walk a few streets to the corner of the popular Ledra Street to find the Shacolas Tower that rises above Debenhams.

Situated on the 11th floor of the Shacolas Tower above Debenhams is the observatory offering panoramic views over the city in all directions including the occupied part of the city with the Pentadactylus mountains in the distance. Entrance costs are low and as well as the views, there is a photographic display recounting events there is an audio account of the 1974 invasion available in a variety of languages.

3. WALK THE CITY WALLS!

Encircling the old part of Nicosia are the star-shaped Venetian walls. The walls are 3 kilometres in length, with 11 bastions and three fortified gates - including the Famagusta Gate which has been carefully renovated and is now a venue for various exhibitions and concerts. There is also a moat although today it is unfilled with water.

To walk the full length of the walls is well worth doing but as part of them lie in the occupied part of the city (have your passport at the ready! At night, the walls are floodlit and look spectacular and they have been the magnificent backdrop to some great summer concerts there in recent years including Elton John and Diana Ross

There are really good walking tours of Old City available from the CTO (Cyprus Tourism Organisation) office in Laiki Yitonia – and they are free of charge.

4. HAVE YOU EVER USED A WOOFAH?

Situated on the outskirts of Nicosia is the Cyprus Handicraft Service workshops which are interesting to visit as all the traditional crafts are represented there – chair making, lace making, candles, copper and weaving. As well as watching the craftspeople at work, it is possible to get involved!

I decided to try my hand at weaving and sat myself at the huge sturdy loom – woofah – and passed the shuttle backwards and forwards as I completed a few rows of a colourful 'Rag Rug'.The aim of CHS is to preserve the crafts of Cyprus, ensuring that they continue to thrive, by teaching them to young people and modifying them to be suitable for modern living.

There is a great retail shop on the site too, but if you can't get to the Nicosia one, there are branches in the main towns.

5. BACK A WINNER!

Nicosia has its own race course which many say is the prettiest horse racing track in Europe! The race course is located at Ayios Dometios and the entrance fees are surprisingly low. It is great fun to watch the races which take place on Wednesdays and Sundays in spring and summer and Wednesdays and Saturdays in autumn and winter. There is no racing in August when the temperatures are too high.

There are ten races on each day and there is the chance to place a small bet – the staff are very helpful and speak several languages and can guide you through the procedure. Even if you don't win, it is nevertheless a great day. If you are staying in Paphos, there are regular trips to the race course from the town.

6. WALK THE WALK

Over recent years, Limassol has definitely grown! Many of the older parts of the town have been sensitively renovated and a broad new promenade which is wheelchair/ pushchair friendly has been constructed that is ideal for families, joggers and friends has been constructed and really is a fun way to exercise.

The walk begins near the town's castle and heads eastwards
  towards the archaeological site of Ancient Amathus and beyond
  to Ayios Tychonas, passing beaches and the gardens of many of
  the island's top hotels. At the beginning of the walk there is a permanent display of modern sculptures and throughout the year there are various markets and exhibitions. There are coffee shops dotted along the way that are perfect for a cold frappé and there are sandy stretches where a quick refreshing dip can be enjoyed too!

7. THE WINE ROUTES.

A fun and slightly different way to explore some of the southwest of Cyprus is to follow a couple of the wine routes! Not only is this a great way to see the country, it's interesting to gain an insight into the long history of wine making in Cyprus and its importance to its economy. Italian archaeologists have confirmed that Cyprus was the first Mediterranean country to make wines and this was as early as 3500 BC.

Cyprus Wine Routes is a really good guide book that is available (free of charge) from branches of the Cyprus Tourism Organisation (CTO). All the wine routes are found in the southwest of Cyprus and a great starting off point for your exploration is the interesting Wine Museum at Erimi (just west of Limassol) which has a cellar and wine tasting too!

8. CAN YOU HEAR THE WHISPER?

The Ancient Theatre at Curium (Kourion) is one of my most favourite places in Cyprus. It was built by the Romans and was once part of a city. It perches high on the cliff tops overlooking the sea with Akrotiri headland in the distance.

Curium is the setting for many events each summer including the annual Shakespeare production in June and a number of music concerts that in the past have ranged from the violinist Vanessa Mae through to the Central Band of the Royal Air Force.

Curium is at its best early in the morning or as the sun sets when there are few people around. The construction of the theatre is impressive, built from numerous huge pieces of limestone that were moved into place by men. The acoustics are perfect and it is possible to stand in the centre of the 'stage' and to whisper and your words will be clearly heard around the theatre - no need for a microphone!

9. DO LOOFAHS GROW?

Close to Limassol Castle is a fascinating museum that is located in an old carob warehouse. The exhibition is all about the two main types of natural sea sponges and how they grow on the seabed and how they are gathered and prepared ready for bath time!

Many years ago, sponge divers weighed down with large stones used to gather the sponges off the coast near Latchi (in the northwest of Cyprus) but sadly the sponges became diseased and could no longer be sold. Visitors to the exhibition also learn all about loofahs and how effective they are for a bath time scrub! Loofahs are actually the fruit of a trailing plant that is grown abundantly in Cyprus, with fruit that looks like a marrow. The museum shop has both bath time companions for sale plus a range of herbal and Dead Sea products which have been proven to be good for the skin.

10. GO VULTURE SPOTTING!

Back in the 1980s the distinctive silhouette of Griffon Vultures in the sky could be seen in 20 different locations in Cyprus but today, sonly one small colony remains – living on the sea cliffs at Episkopi (on the old coastal road between Limassol and Paphos in the Sovereign Base Area).

The vulture is very impressive with brown feathers and black tipped wings. His wingspan measures 2.5 metres and he has disti4nctive ruffle of feathers around the base of the neck. The vultures usually soar above the Episkopi headland late morning and it is great to stop the car for a few minutes and watch them.

There used to be many Griffon vultures in Cyprus because food was plentiful. Vultures feed on dead animals and there were many more donkeys and other animals in the rural areas. Great care is being taken to protect these vultures as they can easily be poisoned by a poisoned carcass they are known to travel many miles in search of food.

Discover The Painted Churches Of Cyprus...

Cyprus has many beautiful Byzantine painted churches and the ten in the Troodos are UNESCO listed. The Painted Churches of Cyprus by Andreas and Judith Stylianou (who are internationally recognised 'as great experts on this subject') explain in their book –

In a large number of rural churches in Cyprus wall paintings have survived which are not only of great value in themselves but also provide a most precious documentation of the development of Byzantine art...

11. RETAIL THERAPY – CYPRUS STYLE!

Whilst all the main towns in Cyprus have a good selection of   shops, it is the markets that are the perfect place to buy top quality fruit and vegetables – and for some great 'people watching'!

There are markets in all the towns and they start really early in the morning. Some of the stalls are large, whilst others are small and run by families selling the produce from their garden. All the produce is incredibly fresh as it will have been gathered the previous evening. There are usually a handful of stalls selling cheese, meat and fish as well as jars of glyka (seasonal fruits that have been preserved in sugar syrup) and leather goods and household linens.

The coffee shop is popular as a small cup of Cyprus Coffee really boosts flagging energy levels and a freshly baked tahinopitta (tahini pastry), spanokopitta (spinach pie) or tyropitta (cheese pie) is the perfect mid-morning treat!

12. GET ENGULFED BY NATURE!

Standing overlooking the Salt Lake is the Akrotiri Environmental, Education and Information Centre. It is a great place to learn all about the peninsula and its 27 different natural habitats – including the wetlands and turtle nesting beaches. 70% of the island's migratory and resident bird species can be found there.

The peninsula has the earliest remains of human civilization that are 12,000 years old.

In the centre there is a variety of exhibits including local basketwork. There are information leaflets and touch screen computers giving access to information on flora, fauna, the geology of the area and the natural habitats. On the first floor there is an observation platform that offers spectacular views of the Salt Lake, Limassol Port and the hill villages of the Limassol area beyond. There are binoculars and a telescope to watch the flamingos and other salt water birds.

13. DO YOU WANT TO STAY YOUNG & BEAUTIFUL?

The beautiful rocks called Petra tou Romiou lie on the island's southern coast, halfway between Paphos and Limassol and is where Aphrodite, the goddess of beauty and love is said to have emerged from the waves in a seashell.

Most visitors to Cyprus love to stop and wander along the beach, but few know of the local legend that tells that if a woman wants to enjoy eternal youth and beauty, she must swim around the furthest rock in the group, three times in an anti-clockwise position. I have made this swim several times but I can't say that it has made a difference yet!

14. HOW SWEET IS YOUR TOOTH?

The road running through the village of Yeroskipou (the Limassol side of Paphos) is lined with shops and a handful of these are making delicious Loukoumia (Cyprus Delights). It is fun to step inside and watch how these sweets are made and of course there are plenty of free samples to enjoy!

Be warned though because the traditional flavour
is rose
water but in recent years many new flavours have
been
added to the range – about 32 in total and much I
like
Loukoumia a sample of each was too much of a
good thing!

Interestingly, the sweet makers also make probably the best sugared almonds in the world with lovely soft coatings that are their natural pale golden colour that simply 'melt in the mouth' – definitely not a place to miss… but don't worry if you are staying in the eastern resorts…there are Loukoumia makers in Kornos and Phini too!

15. PANO OR KATO?

There are a number of pairs of villages, where one has the prefix 'Pano' meaning upper and the other 'Kato' meaning lower. There are two parts to Paphos too – Pano Paphos or Ktima, which is the old town and Kato Paphos with its luxury hotels and restaurants. further down the hill and stretching along the coast from the harbour and Paphos Castle. Both are worth exploring.

Ktima is a maze of narrow shopping streets where you will find all the different craftsmen including a really excellent shoemaker and several tailors who can make you a made-to-measure suit in just days! There are also small pottery and copper shops, jewellers who can design a piece just for you, wonderful traditional tavernas and the market.

Kato Paphos is completely different with a good selection of restaurants serving different international cuisines, the harbour and the town's greatest archaeological treasures – its Roman mosaics. It is the focus for a number of local festivals including Carnival, Kataklysmos and the Green Monday kite flying competitions!

16. EXPLORE A HIDDEN WORLD.

The Avakas Gorge lies on the edge of the Akamas and carves its way down through volcanic rocks and limestone from nearly 700 metres (2,000 ft.) near Kato Arodhes down to sea level.

The gorge is truly a hidden world with 30 metre cliffs forming a steep gully where sunlight rarely penetrates. At one point the gorge is barely two metres wide and the famous 'Hanging Rock' is a huge boulder of coraline limestone that is wedged between the cliffs and hangs precariously above the gorge at this point

After heavy rain the water is funnelled down the gorge at speed -producing flash floods that can raise the water level by several feet in minutes. This is a crucial point to remember for those who plan to explore the gorge in the cooler winter months.

17. TO LOVE OR TO HATE?

The small village of Pano Arodhes is the starting point for the walk down through the Avakas Gorge.

In the centre of the village is the church of Ayios Kelandion which was damaged in the earthquake of 1995. In the courtyard of the church lies two sarcophagi – one of Ayio the other of Ayios Misitikos (the god of hate).

Local folklore tells that to evoke these emotions in someone, a person should secretly scrape some dust from of the stone of the appropriate sarcophagus and slip in to the person's drink and wait for the required effect...

Interestingly, much more stone has been scrapped away from the sarcophagus of Ayios Misitikos...Just outside the village, the water from the well of Ayios Kelandion is credited with curing skin ailments.

18. GET OFF THE BEATEN TRACK!

If you enjoy getting truly off the beaten track and fancy exploring a totally isolated dramatic and ruggedly beautiful part of Cyprus steeped in history and mythology, on foot or in a 4 x 4 drive hire car, then the Akamas peninsula, northwest of Paphos, is definitely for you!

For geology buffs there are dramatic limestone features have been sculptured by the sea and wind and there are volcanic rocks too forced through fissures, millions of years ago into pillow lava.

The Akamas has more than 500 species of plants including wild orchids and sand lilies, but my favourite are the small crimson Akamas tulip {Tulipa cypria} which is native to this area, There is a rich variety of migratory birds and butterflies too.

19. SHE LOVES ME, SHE LOVES ME NOT...

Ayios Yeoryios is a little fishing harbour that lies on the edge of the Akamas peninsula and is best known for its large modern church of Ayios Yeoryios (St George) and good fish taverna.

The islet of Yeronissos lies not far from the shore and in recent years the remains of a Neolithic settlement have been found on its southern side and archaeologists believe that this area used to be a thriving community and important episkopal see as beautiful mosaics – once the floor of a basilica have been uncovered.

Not far from the modern church lies a small chapel that is known locally as 'the church for lovers'. Legend has it that a man should light a candle and point it down to the floor whilst saying the name of his loved one three times...if the candle continues to burn then she really loves him too, but alas if the flame of the candle dies...

20. OPERA UNDER THE STARS!

If you are visiting Cyprus over the first weekend of September, there is only one place to be...Paphos Harbour! For the past 19 years, The Paphos Aphrodite Festival Company has hosted an international opera company to perform one of the much loved operas – in the stunning setting of Paphos Harbour with its magnificent castle as the backdrop.

Even if you are not an opera fan, this event definitely takes opera to a new level with the soloists performing on the stage and fishing boats in the background – their crews oblivious of events in the harbour!

The ticket prices are really reasonably priced and the performances are memorable. The visiting orchestra is often supplemented with musicians from the Cyprus Symphony Orchestra based in Nicosia – a real must do!

Get up close to nature...

Until her death in 2014, Sheila Hawkins was a popular and bestselling writer. Her first book, Back of Beyond told how she and husband, Harry, swapped life in the Royal Air Force for the a rural village on the edge of the Akamas. She loved the local wildlife and this is her description of the colony of Egyptian Fruit Bats that were later visited by David Attenborough.

Suddenly, we found ourselves in a big cave with a ceiling high above our heads. We could hear whisperings and flutterings and squeakings and as our eyes became accustomed to the dark, we could make out the interior walls going back a long way in places. We directed the beam of a powerful flood light upwards and hundreds of fruit bats, huge eyes in their furry faces, were hanging there in groups above us...

© Sheila Hawkins from The Back of Beyond.

21. A VERY SPECIAL CONSERVATION PROJECT

If you have a four wheel drive hire car and you are planning to explore the Akamas, 'the jewel in the crown' is the Turtle Conservation Project at for the Lara-Toxeftra Area which covers 10 kilometres of the Akamas coastline.

The project was begun in 1978 by volunteers from the Fisheries Department who have worked tirelessly ever since trying to stabilise the numbers of Green (Chelonia mydas) and Loggerhead (Caretta caretta) turtles. Their nests are protected by Cypriot law. Since 1995, there has been a tagging programme so that information can be gathered.

On the beach at Lara there is a seasonal information centre with information boards telling the story of this very special conservation project. .

22. HUG THE COAST!

The coastal walk from the Baths of Aphrodite to the furthest tip of the island at Cape Arnaouti is rarely busy, yet is stunningly beautiful in places with views over pebble strewn coves with the clearest water imaginable.

The fig-shrouded Baths of Aphrodite is where Adonis is saw the goddess bathing and fell in love with her – those seeking eternal beauty, must splash their face with water from the pool! The coastal path leads past the Tower of Rigena and the little chapel of St Nikolaos. There are views over the islet of St George before walkers arrive at the tiny Fontana Amorosa (Spring of Love) – again linked to Aphrodite but sadly there are no visible springs today, the water table must have lowered! After a while, the path drops down to sea level and a truly beautiful cove which is perfect for a well-earned swim before the final short distance to the point.

23. HAVE YOU HEARD OF WATERPROOF BASKETS?

Baskets have been made – and used- in Cyprus for centuries and are still made in some villages in the Paphos District and in the village of Inia the museum in the renovated old school building tells the story of basket making...

Before plastic, baskets were used for storing clothes and food as well as shaping cheeses, carrying produce from the market and as wall decorations. Large soft panniers were woven from rushes and fastened on the backs of donkeys for carrying grapes and carobs at harvest time. To make the baskets waterproof they were lined with a layer of mud and then lime so that they could hold wine and olive oil. Purple and green dye was used to decorate the baskets.

The basket museum opened in 1996 as part of an initiative for rural development in the Akamas to revive the local handicrafts and basket makers can often be found at work just outside... and the best news of all is that you can treat yourself to a new basket as there is a well-stocked shop there too!

24. TRY THE CLASSIC CYPRIOT COCKTAIL!

Brandy Sour was first created in the 1930s when the young King Farouk of Egypt visited the Forest Park hotel in Pano Platres. He enjoyed Western cocktails but his Muslim faith prohibited the drinking of alcohol, so the hotel barman created the recipe so that members of the King's entourage thought he was drinking iced tea! If like me, you do not drink spirits, Brandy Sour tastes as good without the Brandy and local bars will happily serve you a 'Sour'!

For one glass of Brandy Sour

I measure of Cyprus Brandy

1 measure of Cyprus lemon squash

Few drops of Angostura Bitters

Chilled soda water

Ice and lemon slices

Pour the lemon squash into a tall glass.

Add the brandy and Angostura Bitters and mix well.

Add the ice cubes and top up with soda and a lemon slice

Stini Yamass- Cheers!

25. STEP INTO YESTERDAY

The little village of Steni lies in the hills between Paphos and Polis Chrysochou and has an amazingly good ethnographical museum that is well worth a visit! Much of the museum has been created by the villagers themselves and often new exhibits are added as they are found in an attic!

The museum reveals local life in the period 1800-1945. There are different sections covering farming, kitchenware, bread making and cloth making and these reveal how self-sufficient the villagers were.

There are several displays including a traditional four poster bed with wax models wearing traditional costumes. It is very much a 'living' museum because in the summer months, some of the village ladies work on the loom in the museum and are happy to let visitors 'have a go'.

26. A REALLY HIDDEN GEM!

Just a short distance from Paphos Airport, on the coastline at Timi, there is a wonderful little know cove with large smooth pebbles and the clearest water imaginable.

The cove is reached by heading towards the airport but where the road from the village swings right towards the airport, take the track to the left, passing the potato fields! There is easy access down to the cove as somebody fixed and old metal spiral staircase there years ago! Best to take a sun umbrella and plenty of sun cream as there is absolutely no shade.

A real bonus is that the aircraft leaving and arriving at Paphos Airport can be clearly seen which is fun for children...

27. BEACHES JUST FOR YOU!

East of the market town of Polis Chrysochou, the road runs through the old copper mines at Limni that gave Cyprus its name and then alongside the deserted sandy beaches for miles .

There are several little fish tavernas right on the beach and the really popular one that overlooks the pretty fishing harbour at Pomos. Beyond Pomos, the scenery becomes very dramatic with steep pine clad hillsides of the Tillyria region. The modern church of Ayios Raphael is particularly beautiful and Packyammos is a huge sandy beach bay. The road is forced into a long 20km detour around the Turkish Kokkina enclave with its abandoned villages. There is a chance to enjoy a good fish meal at Mansoura, or further on at Kato Pyrgos – a bustling market town well known for its fruit.

28. A MOMENT IN TIME

The furthest village along the northern coast before The Green Line is Kato Pyrgos. Four kilometres inland up a twisting, narrow road lies the hamlet of Pano Pyrgos, the centre of one of the country's most important cottage industries - charcoal making.

The charcoal is still made using traditional methods and taking 7-10 days. Wood is brought down from the nearby Tilleria Forest by donkey or tractor, cut into suitable lengths and then built into the characteristic circular domes where the wood smoulders very gently.

As you approach the hamlet there are charcoal kilns on either side of the road. Some of them are ready to be lit; others are gently smouldering and others being carefully dismantled. In the centre of each of these, sits a woman, protected from the sun by a canopy. She sits filling and stitching scores of bags and sacks filled with charcoal that are so instantly recognisable from the piles on sale in all Cypriot supermarkets...

29. WHO'S FOR TAVLI?

A 'must do' during your stay in Cyprus is to enjoy a cup of Cyprus coffee in a traditional coffee shop. In many villages you will find several coffee shops, each one is affiliated to a different political party. The coffee shop remains a male domain and although women are made welcome, it is unusual for women to enter one on their own- the modern style coffee houses are very different!

Cyprus coffee is made in a small long-handled cooking pan known as an imbriki and is thick, strong and served black in a small coffee cup accompanied by a glass of cold water. Coffee made without sugar is known as sketos, whilst medium sweet coffee is metrios and sweet coffee –glykos

The local coffee shop is where the world is put right and certainly a place for lively discussion or a good game of Tavli (backgammon). It is a good source of local information including houses for rent and jobs.

30. FAR FROM THE MADDING CROWD...

The working convent of Ayios Minas is situated not far from the archaeological site of Chirokitia and lace-making village of Pano Lefkara. Ayios Minas is immaculately run by the 13 nuns who live there and it is a wonderful place for private reflection.

The mellow stoned convert was built in the 15th century and was originally a monastery, but the last monks left in 1825 and in fell into disrepair. After some years, the number of women becoming nuns had increased dramatically and the first con vent (at Ayios Yeoryios Alamanas) had more than 60 nuns so renovation work began on Ayios Minas- much of the work was funded by the Cypriot community in London. For those who would like to give a donation towards the upkeep of the convent, there is a small shop where local honey, seasonal fruit and herbs gathered by the nuns can be bought and there are icons and religious books to buy too.

Commandaria – History in a glass...

Lady travellers who visited Cyprus as it was en route between the continents of Europe Africa and Asia. They wrote many detailed notes about the Cypriots, their lives and traditions and many had their work published. In her book Across Cyprus, OM Chapman describes the sweet dessert wine Commandaria which used to be a major export for Cyprus and was drunk in all the courts of Europe and can be bought in supermarkets today...

– The Commandaria, a rich sweet white wine of a deep golden colour which, when darkened with age, resembles old Madeira, owes its name and origin to the Knights Commanders of the Temple who, when in possession of Cyprus at the end of the twelfth

41

century, manufactured it from vines covering the mountain slopes behind Limassol. The fame of Cyprus wine spread throughout Europe, and the demand for it was great. The industry has, a still more remote origin, for Cyprus wines are mentioned in some of the Ancient Greek writings.

31. MOUNTAIN POTS

The mountain village of Phini (Foini) ks well known for its red clay pottery. There were good natural resources closed by and the villagers made a whole range of different sized storage jars – including the huge rounded ones known as pitharia.

The pitharia were made using coils of red clay and once the jar had dried in the sun it would be fired and then lined with lime to make it waterproof. The pitharia were used for storing wine, olive oil and vinegar. The museum in the village is run by Theophanos Pilavakis whose family was one of the main pottery families. In the museum there is a large pithari which has a chair inside, the idea being that a pregnant woman in labour could sit there surrounded by steam to ease her labour pains...

In 2000 Theophanis won a place in The Guinness Book of Records for building the large pithari – a 2,000 litre one!

32. THOUSANDS OF ROSES...

The attractive mountain village of Agros is transformed each May by thousands of deep pink Damascus roses- their fragrance carried on the breeze.

Early each morning a group of women can be found hard at work carefully picking the flower heads before the sun has the chance to evaporate their precious essential oil. The flowers are taken quickly to the rosewater factory, run by Chris and his family, which sits on one of the hillsides where the essential oil will be quickly extracted.

Rose water has been used for generations for both for cooking and beauty in Cyprus! Many of the delicious local pastries such as Baklava and Kadeyfi are flavoured with rosewater whilst many older ladies still use it as an effective skin cleanser and moisturiser that beautifully perfumes the skin too.

33. A SPOONFUL OF GLYKO?

Glyka (plural of glyko) is seasonal fruit that has been preserved in sweet sugar syrup. This method of preservation has been used by Cypriot housewives long before refrigeration and a piece of glyko would traditionally be served on a small plate with an equally small fork to visitors who came to the family home.

There is a large glyka factory on the main Limassol- Platres road (B8) where Katerina and her staff not only make glyka but experiment with new fruit and vegetables each year as well as the popular traditional ones such as orange, cherry, plum – and the most prized, green walnuts! A popular glyko is garlic as it has all the health benefits without the taste or smell! A few years ago Katerina started making glyko from 'prickly pear' – baboutsosika- and this has been particularly popular as tests in Greece have shown that eating prickly pears can help protect men against prostate cancer.

34. HAVE YOU HEARD OF FILFAR?

If you are heading up to the mountains and need to do some souvenir shopping it is a good excuse to stop off at the Filfar Liqueur House in the lovely mountain village of Monagri!

Filfar has a long history and its recipe was bought some years ago by Demos Aristidou. Filfar (original) is a delicious combination of orange juice and local herbs and can be enjoyed either as a liqueur or as a long drink mixed with lemonade or soda. Demos has added three other flavours to the range now – Lemon, Mandarin and Bergemot. There is the chance to see the liqueurs being made and to taste some too!

As well as enjoying Filfar as a drink, dried mixed fruit soaked in Filfar Orange rally does make a great Christmas Cake and Filfar Lemon adds a zing to lemon ice cream...if you do go along you can practise your Greek – stini yamass – cheers!

35. DISCOVER A HIDDEN TREASURE

If you have a hire car and are wanting to discover 'Lesser Known Cyprus' your explorations should include the Xeros Valley – one of three large (mostly) dry river valleys that carve their way down from the Tooodos mountains to the coast near Paphos. The greatest treasure of these valleys can be found nestling on the western bank of the valley of the Potamos Xeros, just below the village of Pentalia. The beautiful monastery of Panayia tou Sinti stands serenely on the grassy banks, protected by the hills behind her, the wind gently whistling through the cobbled courtyard where the monks used to walk. The monastery was built in the 16th century by a young apprentice whilst the Master Builder built one on the opposite bank. The monastery was encircled by a protective wall and dominated by its beautiful church overlooking the large courtyard lined on three sides by the stone buildings that used to be the refectory, kitchen, storage rooms and monastic cells. The peace and solitude there is very special and it is the perfect place to spend some time in quiet reflection...

36. TRULY A NIGHT TO REMEMBER...

Kykko Monastery nestles amidst the mountains and is well worth a visit by day as its church is spectacular, and many of the are covered in gold. Kykko Monastery is the most important in the Orthodox world. It is possible to stay there overnight (although this must be booked well in advance) and there is something so special about joining the monks for their prayers at 04.00.

Close by stands Throni, the highest peak and it is there that the tomb of Archbishop Makarios can be seen –with magnificent views over the mountains and with his home village of Panayia in the distance.

37. SKI THEN SWIM!

The winter season in Cyprus is very short and most days have blue sky and warm sunshine. Nevertheless, the Troodos mountains that are like the central spine of the island, usually get a good dusting of snow.

The summit of Mt Olympus (1,952 metres) is quickly transformed into a ski resort with T bars, downhill runs, langlauf (cross country skiing) routes and the chance to try snowboarding. There is an equipment store for hiring kit and lessons can be booked with ski instructors. The two most important bits of kit though are sunglasses (because of the glare from the snow) and sun tan cream to prevent red noses!

Because Mt Olympus is situated just over an hour's drive from Limassol, it is possible to enjoy a morning's skiing and then drive down to the coast and take an exhilarating swim in the sea!

38. NOT JUST FOR SALADS!

Whilst you are exploring Cyprus you will see countless olive groves. It is said that there is one olive tree for each person in Cyprus! The olives are collected from the trees by beating the branches with poles and collecting the olives on large pieces of netting spread under each tree.

The best quality olive oil to buy is Extra Virgin as it is packed with vitamins and minerals. Certainly it is great to use in the kitchen, but did you know that it is a great beauty product too?

• Ten drops of olive oil in your bath water will leave your skin feeling amazingly soft.

• Mix olive oil and sea salt to create a really efficient
exfoliator.

• To clean really dirty hands, pour a teaspoon of sugar on them and add a tablespoon of olive oil and rub
together – hands will be clean and soft!

39. INSPIRATION FROM THE MOUNTAINS...

The mountain village of Pano Platres is situated on the road up to Troodos and is popular in the summer for its cool clear air and in the winter it is transformed into a skiers' paradise!

Pano Platres was at its most popular in the 1940s and 1950s, when it was much larger (with 15 hotels) and many holiday residences which attracted wealthy traders from Greece and also members of the British

Army serving in Cairo and Alexandria but finding the summer heat unbearable. Many of the men paid for their families to spend the summer in comfort in Pano Platres. In 1936, the novelist Daphne du Maurier stayed at the Forest Park Hotel, whilst he husband Major Browning stayed in Egypt, and it was there that she began writing her popular novel 'My Cousin Rachel'.

40. SQUEAKY CHEESE!

Halloumi is the Cypriot cheese that has been made on the island since medieval times. Halloumi is very distinctive as it is a white, semi-hard cheese that is kept in brine and flavoured with mint. Traditionally, Halloumi has been made with a mixture of sheep and goats' milk and this type of Halloumi can be found in the villages. Halloumi is produced commercially as it is popular all over Europe (especially the U.K) and Middle East and the commercial brands are usually made from cow's milk.

Halloumi is very versatile as it has a high melting point so it can be fried, grilled, or threaded onto skewers and barbecued! The traditional way to eat

Halloumi is cut into cubes with pieces of watermelon, although slices of Halloumi eaten with local Lountza (smoked ham) and tomatoes tastes just as good! Eaten uncooked, the Halloumi has a pleasant slightly rubbery taste and is known to squeak on the teeth!

The Appeal Of Cyprus

Roddy Damalis is a dynamic South African born Cypriot, who is a top Limassol Chef running one of the most popular restaurants in Limassol, has cookery programmes on TV and runs cookery workshops... in his bestselling cook book Ta Piatakia he says-

During the last ten years Cyprus has changed dramatically as it is now a member of the EU. My beloved Limassol is blossoming into a colourful cosmopolitan collage of theatres, restaurants, clubs and culture that is still in touch with nature with coastal walks, migrating flamingos and beautiful mountain scenery. This wonderful town is home to me and many others who draw on its positive energy but contribute to it too. When I close my eyes and think of Cyprus I see so much...

www.roddydamalis.com

41. JOIN A CARAVAN!

In years gone by, the main forms of transport in Cyprus were donkeys and camels. Camels were used to carry important goods to and fro the harbour at Larnaca and would could be seen walking in long lines known as ' camel caravans'. The camels carried woven panniers strapped to their humps and these were filled with copper, carobs and silk which they would transport from the villages to the waiting ships in the harbour.

At the Camel Park in Mazotos it is interesting to see the camels – particularly in the spring and early summer when there are usually young camels too, but there is also the chance to enjoy a ride on a camel either along the shore or in the local countryside – be warned, camels always lower their back legs first!

42. MORE THAN A PINCH OF SALT!

As your aircraft begins its descent into Larnaca Airport, passengers get a spectacular view of the nearby salt lake with the mosque of Hala Sultan Tekke standing on its shores.

There are two salt lakes in Cyprus, the other being at Akrotiri, but salt from the Larnaca lake was a major export for the town for centuries.

During the summer, the layer of salt can be up to 10 cm thick. In the past up to 25,000 tons was exported and a further 4,000 tons used locally for the leather tanning and cheese making industries. The salt was carried in large woven panniers by trains of up to 100 donkeys.

During the winter months, both lakes fill with sea water and
Become the over wintering locations for thousands of beautiful flamingos who feed on the abundant supply of krill in the shallow waters

43. BLUE AMIDST THE RED!

A cluster of villages near Ayia Napa are known as 'Kokkinochoria' meaning 'red soil villages' as the soil really is a deep red colour and extremely fertile. This area produces the famous Cypriot potato. Near the coast, about 14 kilometres southwest of Ayia Napa is the pretty little village of Liopetri which overlooks a long creek where scores of wooden fishing boats are moored.

Much of the time the area is deserted except for the fishermen who can be seen mending their nets and others are busy repainting their boats. It's a popular place for a delicious fish dish as you can't get fresher than this!

44. IT'S IN THE BALANCE!

Cyprus is definitely the place to enjoy good fish and there are numerous fish tavernas strung along the coast. One of the most popular places is Zygi on the old coastal road from Limassol to Larnaca – Zygi is halfway and its name means 'balance'.

There are many different fish and shellfish to enjoy including Sargos (Sea Bream), Barbouni (Red Mullet), Xiphias (Swordfish) and Kalamari (Squid). You can choose the fish you would like to eat from the display cabinet (all prices are per kilo).The fish is simply cooked –usually grilled and served with salad.

If you are unsure of which fish to choose, why not opt for a Fish Mezé (Mezedhes) which is a selection of all the different fish! The dishes are served at a leisurely place with dips, salad and plenty of fresh lemon to drizzle on top! A leisurely meal in Zygi is definitely to be recommended - but never on Sunday when families from Nicosia travel down for a great meal by the sea!

45. DIVE CYPRUS!

The island's coastal waters are incredibly clear with visibility of 10-40 metres and many people take the opportunity of learning to dive during their holiday and experienced divers have more than 50 dive sites to choose from including.

one of the world's top ten dive sites which is situated just one kilometre from the coast in Larnaca...

The Zenobia was a Swedish truck ferry that went down in 1980 on her maiden voyage. She was fully laden with more than with 107 cargo lorries. The top of the Zenobia lies just 16 metres under the waves and all the lorries can still be clearly seen in the wreck and lying on the seabed close by. Most of the lorries are still intact – including an egg lorry complete with cargo!

If you would like to see the wreck but are not a diver, there are mini-submarines that regularly take passengers to visit the wreck and of course to see the shoals of fish in the vicinity!

46. KOPIASTE – COME AND SHARE OUR FOOD...

Good food is always important when visiting a country and Cypriot cuisine is great! Like Greek food is one of the healthiest diets in the world with plenty of fresh fruit, vegetable and olive oil. Cyprus is blessed with fertile land and a walk in the countryside reveals wild herbs including rosemary, thyme and sage. The different fruit and vegetable growing seasons are well defined in Cyprus as only a small portion of food is frozen.

Because the island has been ruled by various countries, each has left its mark – for example, pasta became popular during Italian rule and when Cyprus was a British Crown Colony a Cypriot version of Christmas Cake was created! Most Cypriot dishes are simply cooked and their flavours enhanced by herbs and spices. Much meat and fish is cooked over charcoal. The best way to enjoy a range of traditional seasonal dishes is to order a Mezé (Mezedhes) in a village taverna.

47. CYPRUS = SUNSHINE & SPORT!

For those who enjoy sport, Cyprus is the perfect holiday destination with a rich variety of sports to enjoy. There are several international golf courses to enjoy in the Paphos area and a number of green bowling clubs too. Water sports are widely available including scuba diving (PADI & BSAC courses available), water skiing, jet skiing, wind surfing and surf boarding. There is great fishing too either freshwater or sea fishing excursion. Paragliding and hang gliding are available and flying lessons are keenly priced in Cyprus.

If you enjoy running, the Logicon Cyprus Marathon takes place early in March each year attracting runners from all around the globe and during the island's brief winter spell there are some good (but short) ski slopes in Troodos. If you prefer being a spectator then the Cyprus Rally in June, will definitely be the one for you!

48. FROM CYPRUS WITH LOVE!

High on the list of favourites is the colourful local pottery and lace embroidery. There is copperware on sale in most towns and filigree silver work in Pano Lefkara. Leather tanning was once a major industry but today, beautifully coloured leather is imported from Italy and can be made by craftsmen into a jacket just for you! There are jewellery craftsmen too who can create modern and traditional pieces and you will be delighted with the price! There are attractive clothes for all the family available and beautiful leather5 products including handbags, wallets and belts.

There are plenty of edible treats to pack including Cyprus Delight (Loukoumia) Sugared Almonds, Halloumi and olive oil. There are some excellent

Cypriot wines and brandies on the market and Filfar the locally made liqueur is a good choice too!

If you wish you had a larger suitcase with you – no problem, suitcases are plentiful and really well priced in Cyprus too!

49. CYPRUS THE STEPPING STONE...

If you are spending several weeks in Cyprus it is fun to use the island as a 'stepping stone' to explore other countries too!

This is possible as there are several cruise companies operating from Limassol Port that offer mini cruises at remarkably good prices!

One of the most popular cruises is the two day trip to the Holy Land and another favourite is the cruise to Rhodes where the ship moors within walking distance of the impressive medieval walls that encircle Rhodes town. Other cruises offer passengers the chance to visit other Greek islands including Symi with its beautiful harbor and sponge market and pretty Mykonos with its windmills.

50. IT'S ALL GREEK TO ME!

Well certainly reading Greek will be as the Greek alphabet is completely different, but the English phonetic spelling is now used on many road signs. Most young Cypriots speak really good English and many older Cypriots can speak enough to get by. They love it if you have a go, here are the key words written phonetically...

Good day	Kalimera (Until about 12.00 p.m.)
Good evening	Kalispera (from 12.00p.m. till late!)
Goodnight	Kalinichta (as you bid farewell & go home)
Yes	Neh
No	Ohi
Please	Parakalo
Thank you	Efharisto
Are you well?	Ee-sas-teh kala? (formal) Ee-seh kala (informal)
What time is it?	Ti ora ee-neh?
Where is (it)?	Poo einai? (the airport - to aero-thromio)

TOP REASONS TO BOOK THIS TRIP

- Beaches: There are all types of beaches, sandy, rocky, ones for lazing and ones for great water sports. beaches here are the best.
- Food: The food in Cyprus is delicious and derived from the island's history.
- Wine: Cyprus has a long history of wine making
- Island Culture: A rich heritage of traditions including music, handicrafts and colourful festivals
- Wildlife: There are so many different wild flowers, birds, mammals and butterflies to see.
- The most important reason of all is the Cypriots who are renowned for their warm hospitality…

BONUS BOOK

50 THINGS TO KNOW ABOUT PACKING LIGHT FOR TRAVEL

PACK THE RIGHT WAY EVERY TIME

AUTHOR: MANIDIPA BHATTACHARYYA

Edited by Melanie Howthorne

ABOUT THE AUTHOR

Manidipa Bhattacharyya is a creative writer and editor, with an education in English literature and Linguistics. After working in the IT industry for seven long years she decided to call it quits and follow her heart instead. Manidipa has been ghost writing, editing, proof reading and doing secondary research services for many story tellers and article writers for about three years. She stays in Kolkata, India with her husband and a busy two year old. In her own time Manidipa enjoys travelling, photography and writing flash fiction.

Manidipa believes in travelling light and never carries anything that she couldn't haul herself on a trip. However, travelling with her child changed the scenario. She seemed to carry the entire world with her for the baby on the first two trips. But good sense prevailed and she is again working her way to becoming a light traveler, this time with a kid.

INTRODUCTION

He who would travel happily
must travel light.

-Antoine de Saint-Exupéry

Travel takes you to different places from seas and mountains to deserts and much more. In your travels you get to interact with different people and their cultures. You will, however, enjoy the sights and interact positively with these new people even more, if you are travelling light.

When you travel light your mind can be free from worry about your belongings. You do not have to spend precious vacation time waiting for your luggage to arrive after a long flight. There is be no chance of your bags going missing and the best part is that you need not pay a fee for checked baggage.

People who have mastered this art of packing light will root for you to take only one carry-on, wherever you go. However, many people can find it really hard to pack light. More so if you are travelling with children. Differentiating between "must have" and "just in case" items is the starting point. There will be ample shopping avenues at your destination which are just waiting to be explored.

This book will show you 'packing' in a new 'light' – pun intended – and help you to embrace light packing practices for all of your future travels.

Off to packing!

DEDICATION

I dedicate this book to all the travel buffs that I know, who have given me great insights into the contents of their backpacks.

THE RIGHT TRAVEL GEAR

1. CHOOSE YOUR TRAVEL GEAR CAREFULLY

While selecting your travel gear, pick items that are light weight, durable and most importantly, easy to carry. There are cases with wheels so you can drag them along – these are usually on the heavy side because of the trolley. Alternatively a backpack that you can carry comfortably on your back, or even a duffel bag that you can carry easily by hand or sling across your body are also great options. Whatever you choose, one thing to keep in mind is that the luggage itself should not weigh a ton, this will give you the flexibility to bring along one extra pair of shoes if you so desire.

2. CARRY THE MINIMUM NUMBER OF BAGS

Selecting light weight luggage is not everything. You need to restrict the number of bags you carry as well. One carry-on size bag is ideal for light travel. Most carriers allow one cabin baggage plus one purse, handbag or camera bag as long as it slides under the seat in front. So technically, you can carry two items of luggage without checking them in.

3. PACK ONE EXTRA BAG

Always pack one extra empty bag along with your essential items. This could be a very light weight duffel bag or even a sturdy tote bag which takes up minimal space. In the event that you end up buying a lot of souvenirs, you already have a handy bag to stuff all that into and do not have to spend time hunting for an appropriate bag.

I'm very strict with my packing and have everything in its right place. I never change a rule. I hardly use anything in the hotel room. I wheel my own wardrobe in and that's it.

Charlie Watts

CLOTHES & ACCESSORIES

4. PLAN AHEAD

Figure out in advance what you plan to do on your trip. That will help you to pick that one dress you need for the occasion. If you are going to attend a wedding then you have to carry formal wear. If not, you can ditch the gown for something lighter that will be comfortable during long walks or on the beach.

5. WEAR THAT JACKET

Remember that wearing items will not add extra luggage for your air travel. So wear that bulky jacket that you plan to carry for your trip. This saves space and can also help keep you warm during the chilly flight.

6. MIX AND MATCH

Carry clothes that can be interchangeably used to reinvent your look. Find one top that goes well with a couple of pairs of pants or skirts. Use tops, shirts and jackets wisely along with other accessories like a scarf or a stole to create a new look.

7. CHOOSE YOUR FABRIC WISELY

Stuffing clothes in cramped bags definitely takes its toll which results in wrinkles. It is best to carry wrinkle free, synthetic clothes or merino tops. This will eliminate the need for that small iron you usually bring along.

8. DITCH CLOTHES PACK UNDERWEAR

Pack more underwear and socks. These are the things that will give you a fresh feel even if you do not get a chance to wear fresh clothes. Moreover these are easy to wash and can be dried inside the hotel room itself.

9. CHOOSE DARK OVER LIGHT

While picking your clothes choose dark coloured ones. They are easy to colour coordinate and can last longer before needing a wash. Accidental food spills and dirt from the road are less visible on darker clothes.

10. WEAR YOUR JEANS

Take only one pair of Jeans with you, which you should wear on the flight. Remember to pick a pair that can be worn for sightseeing trips and is equally eloquent for dinner. You can add variety by adding light weight cargoes and chinos.

11. CARRY SMART ACCESSORIES

The right accessory can give you a fresh look even with the same old dress. An intelligent neck-piece, a couple of bright scarves, stoles or a sarong can be used in a number of ways to add variety to your clothing. These light weight beauties can double up as a nursing cover, a light blanket, beach wear, a modesty cover for visiting places of worship, and also makes for an enthralling game of peek-a-boo.

12. LEARN TO FOLD YOUR GARMENTS

Seasoned travellers all swear by rolling their clothes for compact and wrinkle free packing. Bundle packing, where you roll the clothes around a central object as if tying it up, is also a popular method of compact and wrinkle free packing. Stacking folded clothes one on top of another is a big no-no as it makes creases extreme and they are difficult to get rid of without ironing.

13. WASH YOUR DIRTY LAUNDRY

One of the ways to avoid carrying loads of clothes is to wash the clothes you carry. At some places you might get to use the laundry services or a Laundromat but if you are in a pinch, best solution is to wash them yourself. If that is the plan then carrying quick drying clothes is highly recommended, which most often also happen to be the wrinkle free variety.

14. LEAVE THOSE TOWELS BEHIND

Regular towels take up a lot of space, are heavy and take ages to dry out. If you are staying at hotels they will provide you with towels anyway. If you are travelling to a remote place, where the availability of towels look doubtful, carry a light weight travel towel of viscose material to do the job.

15. USE A COMPRESSION BAG

Compression bags are getting lots of recommendation now days from regular travellers. These are useful for saving space in your luggage when you have to pack bulky dresses. While packing for the return trip, get help from the hotel staff to arrange a vacuum cleaner.

FOOTWEAR

16. PUT ON YOUR HIKING BOOTS

If you have plans to go hiking or trekking during your trip, you will need those bulky hiking boots. The best way to carry them is to wear them on flight to save space and luggage weight. You can remove the boots once inside and be comfortable in your socks.

17. PICKING THE RIGHT SHOES

Shoes are often the bulkiest items, along with being the dainty if you are a female. They need care and take up a lot of space in your luggage. It is advisable therefore to pick shoes very carefully. If you plan to do a lot of walking and site seeing, then wearing a pair of comfortable walking shoes are a must. For more formal occasions you can carry durable, light weight flats which will not take up much space.

18. STUFF SHOES

If you happen to pack a pair of shoes, ensure you utilize their hollow insides. Tuck small items like rolled up socks or belts to save space. They will also be easy to find.

TOILETRIES

19. STASHING TOILETRIES

Carry only absolute necessities. Airline rules dictate that for one carry-on bag, liquids and gels must be in 3.4 ounce (100ml) bottles or less, and must be packed in a one quart zip-lock bag. If you are planning to stay in a hotel, the basic things will be provided for you. It's best is to buy the rest from the local market at your destination.

20. TAKE ALONG TAMPONS

Tampons are a hard to find item in a lot of countries. Figure out how many you need and pack accordingly. For longer stays you can buy them online and have them delivered to where you are staying.

21. GET PAMPERED BEFORE YOU TRAVEL

Some avid travellers suggest getting a pedicure and manicure just the day before travelling. This not only gives you a well kept look, you also save the trouble of packing nail polish. Remember, every little bit of weight reduced adds up.

ELECTRONICS

22. LUGGING ALONG ELECTRONICS

Electronics have a large role to play in our lives today. Most of us cannot imagine our lives away from our phones, laptops or tablets. However while travelling, one must consider the amount of weight these electronics add to our luggage. Thankfully smart phones come along with all the essentials tools like a camera, email access, picture editing tools and more. They are smart to the point of eliminating the need to carry multiple gadgets. Choose a smart phone that suits all your requirements and travel with the world in your palms or pocket.

23. REDUCE THE NUMBER OF CHARGERS

If you do travel with multiple electronic devices, you will have to bear the additional burden of carrying all their chargers too. Check if a single charger can be used for multiple devices. You might also consider investing in a pocket charger. These small devices support multiple devices while keeping you charged on the go.

24. TRAVEL FRIENDLY APPS

Along with smart phones come numerous apps, which are immensely helpful in our travels. You name it and you have an app for it at hand – take pictures, sharing with friends and family, torch to light dark roads, maps, checking flight/train times, find hotels and many other things. Use these smart alternatives to traditional items like books to eliminate weight and save space.

I get ideas about what's essential when packing my suitcase.

-Diane von Furstenberg

TRAVELLING WITH KIDS

25. BRING ALONG THE STROLLER

Kids might enjoy walking for a while but they soon tire out and a stroller is the just the right thing for them to rest in while you continue your tour. Strollers also double duty as a luggage carrier and shopping bag holder. Remember to pick a light weight, easy to handle brand of stroller. Better yet, find out in advance if you can rent a stroller at your destination.

26. BRING ONLY ENOUGH DIAPERS FOR YOUR TRIP

Diapers take up a lot of space and add to the weight of your luggage. Therefore it is advisable to carry just enough diapers to last through the trip and a few for afterwards, till you buy fresh stock at your destination. Unless of course you are travelling to a really remote area, in which case you have no choice but to carry the load. Otherwise diapers are something you will find pretty easily.

27. TAKE ONLY A COUPLE OF TOYS

Children are easily attracted by new things in their environment. While travelling they will find numerous 'new' objects to scrutinize and play with. Packing just one favorite toy is enough, or if there is no favorite toy leave out all of them in favor of stories or imaginary games.

28. CARRY KID FRIENDLY SNACKS

Create a small snack counter in your bag to store away quick bites for those sudden hunger pangs. Depending on the child's age this could include chocolates, raisins, dry fruits, granola bars or biscuits. Also keep a bottle of water handy for your little one. These things do not add much weight and can be adjusted in a handbag or knapsack.

29. GAMES TO CARRY

Create some travel specific, imaginary games if you have slightly grown up children, like spot the attractions. Keep a coloring book and colors handy for in-flight or hotel time. Apps on your smart phone can keep the children engaged with cartoons and story books. Older children are often entertained by games available on phones or tablets. This cuts the weight of luggage down while keeping the kids entertained.

30. LET THE KIDS CARRY THEIR LOAD

A good thing is to start early sharing of responsibilities. Let your child pick a bag of his or her choice and pack it themselves. Keep tabs on what they are stuffing in their bags by asking if they will be using that item on the trip. It could start out being just an entertainment bag initially but with growing years they will learn to sort the useful from the superfluous. Children as little as four can maneuver a small trolley suitcase like a pro- their experience in pull along toys credit. If you are worried that you may be pulling it for them, you may want to start with a backpack.

31. DECIDE ON LOCATION FOR CHILDREN TO SLEEP

While on a trip you might not always get a crib at your destination, and carrying one will make life all the more difficult. Instead call ahead to see if there are any cribs or roll out beds for children. You may even put blankets on the floor. Weave them a story about camping and they will gladly sleep without any trouble.

32. GET BABY PRODUCTS DELIVERED AT YOUR DESTINATION

If you are absolutely paranoid about not getting your favourite variety of diaper or brand of baby food, check out online stores like amazon.com for services in your destination city. You can buy things online ahead of your travel and get them delivered to your hotel upon arrival.

33. FEEDING NEEDS OF YOUR INFANTS

If you are travelling with a breastfed infant, you save the trouble of carrying bottles and bottle sanitization kits. For special food, or medications, you may need to call ahead to make sure you have a refrigerator where you are staying.

34. FEEDING NEEDS OF YOUR TODDLER

With the progression from infancy to toddler, their dietary requirements too evolve. You will have to pack some snacks for travelling time. Fresh fruits and vegetables can be purchased at your destination. Most of the cities you travel to in whichever part of the world, will have baby food products and formulas, available at the local drug-store or the supermarket.

35. PICKING CLOTHES FOR YOUR BABY

Contrary to popular belief, babies can do without many changes of clothes. At the most pack 2 outfits per day. Pack mix and match type clothes for your little one as well. Pick things which are comfortable to wear and quick to dry.

36. SELECTING SHOES FOR YOUR BABY

Like outfits, kids can make do with two pairs of comfortable shoes. If you can get some water resistant shoes it will be best. To expedite drying wet shoes, you can stuff newspaper in them then wrap them with newspaper and leave them to dry overnight.

37. KEEP ONE CHANGE OF CLOTHES HANDY

Travelling with kids can be tricky. Keep a change of clothes for the kids and mum handy in your purse or tote bag. This takes a bit of space in your hand luggage but comes extremely handy in case there are any accidents or spills.

38. LEAVE BEHIND BABY ACCESSORIES

Baby accessories like their bed, bath tub, car seat, crib etc. should be left at home. Many hotels provide a crib on request, while car seats can be borrowed from friends or rented. Babies can be given a bath in the hotel sink or even in the adult bath tub with a little bit of water. If you bring a few bath toys, they can be used in the bath, pool, and out of water. They can also be sanitized easily in the sink.

39. CARRY A SMALL LOAD OF PLASTIC BAGS

With children around there are chances of a number of soiled clothes and diapers. These plastic bags help to sort the dirt from the clean inside your big bag. These are very light weight and come in handy to other carry stuff as well at times.

PACK WITH A PURPOSE

40. PACKING FOR BUSINESS TRIPS

One neutral-colored suit should suffice. It can be paired with different shirts, ties and accessories for different occasions. One pair of black suit pants could be worn with a matching jacket for the office or with a snazzy top for dinner.

41. PACKING FOR A CRUISE

Most cruises have formal dinners, and that formal dress usually takes up a lot of space. However you might find a tuxedo to rent. For women, a short black dress with multiple accessory options will do the trick.

42. PACKING FOR A LONG TRIP OVER DIFFERENT CLIMATES

The secret packing mantra for travel over multiple climates is layering. Layering traps air around your body creating insulation against the cold. The same light t-shirt that is comfortable in a warmer climate can be the innermost layer in a colder climate.

REDUCE SOME MORE WEIGHT

43. LEAVE PRECIOUS THINGS AT HOME

Things that you would hate to lose or get damaged leave them at home. Precious jewelry, expensive gadgets or dresses, could be anything. You will not require these on your trip. Leave them at home and spare the load on your mind.

44. SEND SOUVENIRS BY MAIL

If you have spent all your money on purchasing souvenirs, carrying them back in the same bag that you brought along would be difficult. Either pack everything in another bag and check it in the airport or get everything shipped to your home. Use an international carrier for a secure transit, but this could be more expensive than the checking fees at the airport.

45. AVOID CARRYING BOOKS

Books equal to weight. There are many reading apps which you can download on your smart phone or tab. Plus there are gadgets like Kindle and Nook that are thinner and lighter alternatives to your regular book.

CHECK, GET, SET, CHECK AGAIN

46. STRATEGIZE BEFORE PACKING

Create a travel list and prepare all that you think you need to carry along. Keep everything on your bed or floor before packing and then think through once again – do I really need that? Any item that meets this question can be avoided. Remove whatever you don't really need and pack the rest.

47. TEST YOUR LUGGAGE

Once you have fully packed for the trip take a test trip with your luggage. Take your bags and go to town for window shopping for an hour. If you enjoy your hour long trip it is good to go, if not, go home and reduce the load some more. Repeat this test till you hit the right weight.

48. ADD A ROLL OF DUCT TAPE

You might wonder why, when this book has been talking about reducing stuff, we're suddenly asking you to pack something totally unusual. This is because when you have limited supplies, duct tape is immensely helpful for small repairs – a broken bag, leaking zip-lock bag, broken sunglasses, you name it and duct tape can fix it, temporarily.

49. LIST OF ESSENTIAL ITEMS

Even though the emphasis is on packing light, there are things which have to be carried for any trip. Here is our list of essentials:

• Passport/Visa or any other ID

• Any other paper work that might be required on a trip like permits, hotel reservation confirmations etc.

• Medicines – all your prescription medicines and emergency kit, especially if you are travelling with children

• Medical or vaccination records

• Money in foreign currency if travelling to a different country

• Tickets- Email or Message them to your phone

50. MAKE THE MOST OF YOUR TRIP

Wherever you are going, whatever you hope to do we encourage you to embrace it whole-heartedly. Take in the scenery, the culture and above all, enjoy your time away from home.

On a long journey even a straw weighs heavy.

-Spanish Proverb

PACKING AND PLANNING TIPS

A Week before Leaving

- Arrange for someone to take care of pets and water plants.

- Stop mail and newspaper.

- Notify Credit Card companies where you are going.

- Change your thermostat settings.

- Car inspected, oil is changed, and tires have the correct pressure.

- Passports and photo identification is up to date.

- Pay bills.

- Copy important items and download travel Apps.

- Start collecting small bills for tips.

Right Before Leaving

- Clean out refrigerator.

- Empty garbage cans.

- Lock windows.

- Make sure you have the proper identification with you.

- Bring cash for tips.

- Remember travel documents.

- Lock door behind you.

- Remember wallet.

- Unplug items in house and pack chargers.

>TOURIST

READ OTHER
GREATER THAN A TOURIST
BOOKS

Greater Than a Tourist San Miguel de Allende Guanajuato Mexico:
50 Travel Tips from a Local by Tom Peterson

Greater Than a Tourist – Lake George Area New York USA:
 50 Travel Tips from a Local by Janine Hirschklau

Greater Than a Tourist – Monterey California United States:
50 Travel Tips from a Local by Katie Begley

 Greater Than a Tourist – Chanai Crete Greece:
50 Travel Tips from a Local by Dimitra Papagrigoraki

Greater Than a Tourist – The Garden Route Western Cape Province
South Africa: 50 Travel Tips from a Local by Li-Anne McGregor van
Aardt

Greater Than a Tourist – Sevilla Andalusia Spain:
50 Travel Tips from a Local by Gabi Gazon

Greater Than a Tourist – Kota Bharu Kelantan Malaysia:
50 Travel Tips from a Local by Aditi Shukla

Children's Book: Charlie the Cavalier Travels the World by Lisa
Rusczyk

> TOURIST

Visit *Greater Than a Tourist* for Free Travel Tips
http://GreaterThanATourist.com

Sign up for the *Greater Than a Tourist* Newsletter for discount days, new books, and travel information:
http://eepurl.com/cxspyf

Follow us on Facebook for tips, images, and ideas:
https://www.facebook.com/GreaterThanATourist

Follow us on Pinterest for travel tips and ideas:
http://pinterest.com/GreaterThanATourist

Follow us on Instagram for beautiful travel images:
http://Instagram.com/GreaterThanATourist

> TOURIST

At *Greater Than a Tourist*, we love to share travel tips with you. How did we do? What guidance do you have for how we can give you better advice for your next trip? Please send your feedback to GreaterThanaTourist@gmail.com as we continue to improve the series. We appreciate your constructive feedback. Thank you.

METRIC CONVERSIONS

TEMPERATURE

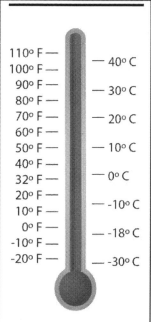

110° F —   — 40° C
100° F —
90° F —   — 30° C
80° F —
70° F —   — 20° C
60° F —
50° F —   — 10° C
40° F —
32° F —   — 0° C
20° F —
10° F —   — -10° C
0° F —
-10° F —   — -18° C
-20° F —   — -30° C

To convert F to C:

Subtract 32, and then multiply
by 5/9 or .5555.

To Convert C to F:

Multiply by 1.8
and then add 32.

32F = 0C

LIQUID VOLUME

To Convert:...................Multiply by
U.S. Gallons to Liters................ 3.8
U.S. Liters to Gallons 26
Imperial Gallons to U.S. Gallons 1.2
Imperial Gallons to Liters........ 4.55
Liters to Imperial Gallons 22
1 Liter = .26 U.S. Gallon
1 U.S. Gallon = 3.8 Liters

DISTANCE

To convert ....Multiply by
Inches to Centimeters 2.54
Centimeters to Inches 39
Feet to Meters...................... .3
Meters to Feet 3.28
Yards to Meters 91
Meters to Yards 1.09
Miles to Kilometers 1.61
Kilometers to Miles............ .62
1 Mile = 1.6 km
1 km = .62 Miles

WEIGHT

1 Ounce = .28 Grams
1 Pound = .4555 Kilograms
1 Gram = .04 Ounce
1 Kilogram = 2.2 Pounds

TRAVEL QUESTIONS

- Do you bring presents home to family or friends after a vacation?

- Do you get motion sick?

- Do you have a favorite billboard?

- Do you know what to do if there is a flat tire?

- Do you like a sun roof open?

- Do you like to eat in the car?

- Do you like to wear sun glasses in the car?

- Do you like toppings on your ice cream?

- Do you use public bathrooms?

- Did you bring your cell phone and does it have power?

- Do you have a form of identification with you?

- Have you ever been pulled over by a cop?

- Have you ever given money to a stranger on a road trip?

- Have you ever taken a road trip with animals?

- Have you ever went on a vacation alone?

- Have you ever run out of gas?

- If you could move to any place in the world, where would it be?

- If you could travel anywhere in the world, where would you travel?

- If you could travel in any vehicle, which one would it be?

- If you had three things to wish for from a magic genie, what would they be?

- If you have a driver's license, how many times did it take you to pass the test?

- What are you the most afraid of on vacation?

- What do you want to get away from the most when you are on vacation?

- What foods smells bad to you?

- What item do you bring on ever trip with you away from home?

- What makes you sleepy?

- What song would you love to hear on the radio when you're cruising on the highway?

- What travel job would you want the least?

- What will you miss most while you are away from home?

- What is something you always wanted to try?

- What is the best road side attraction that you ever saw?

- What is the farthest distance you ever biked?

- What is the farthest distance you ever walked?

- What is the weirdest thing you needed to buy while on vacation?

- What is your favorite candy?

- What is your favorite color car?

- What is your favorite family vacation?

- What is your favorite food?

- What is your favorite gas station drink or food?

- What is your favorite license plate design?

- What is your favorite restaurant?

- What is your favorite smell?

- What is your favorite song?

- What is your favorite sound that nature makes?

- What is your favorite thing to bring home from a vacation?

- What is your favorite vacation with friends?

- What is your favorite way to relax?

- Where is the farthest place you ever traveled in a car?

- Where is the farthest place you ever went North, South, East and West?

- Where is your favorite place in the world?

- Who is your favorite singer?

- Who taught you how to drive?

- Who will you miss the most while you are away?

- Who if the first person you will contact when you get to your destination?

- Who brought you on your first vacation?

- Who likes to travel the most in your life?

- Would you rather be hot or cold?

- Would you rather drive above, below, or at the speed limited?

- Would you rather drive on a highway or a back road?

- Would you rather go on a train or a boat?

- Would you rather go to the beach or the woods?

TRAVEL BUCKET LIST

1.

2.

3.

4.

5.

6.

7.

8.

9.

10.

NOTES

43515593R00068

Made in the USA
Middletown, DE
25 April 2019